The Chi Key

J Pilgrim

Published by Xcel Wellness, 2024.

While every precaution has been taken in the preparation of this book, the publisher assumes no responsibility for errors or omissions, or for damages resulting from the use of the information contained herein.

THE CHI KEY

First edition. January 2, 2024.

Copyright © 2024 J Pilgrim.

ISBN: 979-8223372905

Written by J Pilgrim.

Also by J Pilgrim

The Trionian Saga
The Trionian Saga - Part One: Beyond the Border Mountains
The Trionian Saga - Part Two: The Hyna Sword
The Trionian Saga - Part Three: The Quest for Lyla
Kass Balou

Standalone
The Hens in Poultsville
Sleeping with Crystal
Excel Your Wellness: Virtues and Vitamins
The Chi Key
Body Strengthening Strategy
Xcel Wellness Tai Chi
The Trionian Saga
Sherleaf
Endless Waterfall

Watch for more at www.thetrioniansaga.weebly.com.

Table of Contents

Unlock the Mysteries of Existence with "The Chi Key"!

Are you troubled by the shadows of uncertainty? Do the mysteries of the cosmos leave you perplexed? Fear not! Within these pages lies a revelation—a beacon of light to guide you through the cosmic labyrinth.

The Chi Key awaits. Step into the cosmic dance.

Are you anxious about your own future? I want to explore a matter that has taken me years to understand and will try to summarize in this publication, potentially replacing your anxiety with peace and confidence. As for you, you may have held onto a belief system for decades—one that is deeply ingrained in your mind and influences every attitude, decision, and action in your life. There might be initial resistance to the ideas in this book, but with an open mind and time, the universe will affirm this original and solid belief system for you. I ask that you carefully consider every point before you.

In this publication, I will give you the CHI KEY. Obtaining this key has cost me money, time, and effort, but I am sharing this mind-blowing information with you at a fraction of the cost. This key will reveal to you how you tick, how other people tick, how the world ticks, and how the universe ticks. It's incredible knowledge to have, and YOU CAN KNOW IT TODAY!

<u>Knowing this information offers the following potential benefits:</u>

- A sense of peace in every challenge and stage of life

- **The assurance that all is well for you in the afterlife**

- Freedom from limited and limiting belief systems

- **Escape from patterns of negative thought and depressive emotional cycles**

- The transparency of mind to understand the mysteries of life's events

- Enhanced relationships through the awareness of how people function

- The stimulus to embrace a foundational and transformative self-love

- Belief in a body of truth that fits perfectly with intuition and life's experiences

Knowledge is Power and Power Changes Ones Destiny in any Sphere of Life.

Your Cosmic Toolbox.

Read "The Chi Key": It's more than a book—it's your stardust guide. Life's instruction manual awaits.

Understand, Unleash: The universe pulses within you. Unleash your potential, for you are woven from cosmic threads.

Definitions

In the following outline of material, I refer to Judaism, Christianity, and Offshoots (JCO). This includes these two religious lineages and their descendants or similar structures with limited and restrictive belief systems. (Note that within these groups, there will be individual and collective exceptions to the rules.) Additionally, in this book, the points discussed may also touch on the political realm if there is a limited and restrictive belief system that excessively subjugates its citizens.

Furthermore, in this outline, I also mention the body of truth known by various names throughout history worldwide, such as Daoism, New Age, and astrology. However, I prefer to call this belief system Universalism (UNI), meaning the Universe is the central intelligent power.

The Collins Dictionary provides this simplified definition: Universe – all existing things regarded as a systematic whole; the world. Universal: relating to all things or all people.

According to the Urban Dictionary, 'Universalism aka "The Universal Truth" is the awareness that all things are interconnected; that all pursuits should aim for the good of people to preserve the natural order of existence. It does not support or oppose the belief in god(s), but if such exists, it is part of The Universal Truth. Regarding religions, all are simply different paths to the same destination. Universalism sees that all humanity and life are connected through a cosmic tapestry, meant to exist in harmony with nature.

Universalism is as old as humanity; it has no limits and can't be confined. Just as waves roll onto the shore, this principle spreads across the cosmos.

In this book, we discuss the Chakras (meaning wheels). These are seven major energy centers along the mid-line of the body that reflect health and spiritual well-being. These Chakras act like multi-dimensional gateways, enabling individuals to access different experiences and consciousness states. Stress in different areas of life can block the flow of energy in certain chakras, leading to imbalance and dis-ease.

Summary of My Life Journey

Before I outline the life-changing points in the following chapters, let me first share a summary of my extraordinary journey.

I was raised in a nominally religious home that was moral, ethical, and grounded. Growing up on a farm, I was close to nature every day. This was my lot for the first eighteen years of my life, and during that time, the focus was on <u>family</u>.

After I left home and moved into the city, I joined a conservative church group and became deeply committed to this strong belief system during the second set of eighteen years, during which my focus was on the <u>Church</u>. In this book, I draw from my background and make comparisons.

During the third eighteen-year period focused on <u>Arts</u>, I grew internally, graduating into my current belief system that the Universe has guided me to through enlightenment, leading to a form of 'gnostic' understanding.

This belief system goes by various names throughout history worldwide, but I prefer to call it Universalism, meaning the Universe is the central intelligent power. Read on to learn more.

Where to Look

JCO programs people to depend on others, to look outside themselves for salvation, deliverance, assurance, and love; and this outward reliance plays into the hands of the clergy to maintain power over the congregation. It's all about power and control in religion and politics, and the one who is positioned as the go-between has the upper hand. This creates a platform for manipulating followers like lemmings heading toward a cliff. Historically, JCO has been used to manipulate individuals and crowds into blind submission, giving power to a few at the top to fulfill their agenda. The malevolence of such a system lies in how each person of Light surrenders their own innate authority to robed priests, believing this is the way to find salvation and Light. This deception often involves sincere belief from both parties. People trapped in cults and fundamentalist beliefs are prevented from truly knowing, expressing, and being themselves, which is both sad and harmful to any angelic being. In these circles, seeking love and salvation within oneself is discouraged, condemned, and warned against. Although JCO has had centuries to craft a message of love, its darker side fosters fear, suppressing the original divine principle and denying that we are pure spirit.

A long-standing subconscious fear is damaging to our health and well-being, and as a massage practitioner, I see how this fear manifests in the bodies, emotions, and minds of my clients.

The original truth is this: we are divine, pure spirits floating in the universe until the moment we are conceived in a woman's womb in a country on this earth. Our higher ego is downloaded—without inherent darkness—into a womb of darkness, developing into a functioning body to be born, allowing us to grow in life until our body returns to dust.

Thus, the cycle continues. In this truth, there is no fear principle, no condemnation, and no need to hand over the reins to someone else.

JCO does not want this original truth to be revealed or JCO risks losing control over the individual and the masses. Therefore, both religion and politics tightly control the official textbooks to distribute creeds, laws, warnings, and penalties, preventing large-scale defiance.

It appears that we are now living in an era where people are gradually awakening to their rights as beings of Light and are reclaiming their rightful sceptres, adorning themselves with golden robes and crowning themselves with crystal brilliance. UNI advises looking inward to find answers to life's questions. Turn to the inner child to discover solutions to learned patterns of unkind behaviour (which begins with being untrue to oneself). Seek the higher self for divine love, acceptance, and security. This is true salvation and keeps power in the right hands.

People are in Life Stages

People go through different life chapters, stages, or parts. What may be exciting this decade for someone might become dull in the next ten years; what attracted attention during their twenties may be replaced by a new cause in their thirties. Those who once belonged to a parish, club, sports team, career, city, or country might no longer be part of those anymore. They have moved on with their lives and entered a new stage.

JCO can use manipulative peer pressure and guilt to intimidate anyone who dares to leave their group. People can be harsh to each other; close friends may turn into enemies overnight when the truth about a member's desire to leave the fold is revealed. History shows many broken promises, friendships, and hearts. This kind of thinking by church members has led to many casualties—well-meaning people trying to convince others to stay in what they feel is right in their hearts.

People are in different life chapters or stages, and this should be acknowledged. No one should be guilt-tripped for seeking change. If it were otherwise, the world would be a much more liveable place. Harmony in relationships would flourish, and positivity could create a brighter future.

One Perspective

JCO tells its followers that those outside their group are ungodly, meaning they have turned their back on God. This is not true, as they do have a God; they believe in a deity or deities. It is just not the same understanding of JCO's God. The Holy Bible's God is the perspective of Jews, Christians, and their offshoots on the Supreme Being. This is their worldview. The judgment they mention is based on their philosophy, and it is their reality, but that may just be one piece in the larger puzzle of universal knowledge. The Jews and Christians have claimed a monopoly on the 'Truth' and considered themselves superior to other segments of society.

UNI states that everyone is on equal footing and that we are all part of nature and the universal whole. We should therefore strive for peace and harmony with one another and learn to redirect conflicting energy into nothingness.

Christianity is not the only reality – it is one aspect of the broader spectrum of world faiths. All belief systems are valid for the cultures that developed or adopted them. Each creed reflects what society's seers promoted, shaping their collective realism. The key point is that any belief system nurtures the Pure Spirit. It's less about following religious rules or sacraments and more about maintaining an unpolluted human spirit in everyday life.

To clarify, it's not about sects or denominations but about connecting to a higher, pure self. We all originate from the Universal Consciousness, conceived and born into this world with an untainted spirit. Whether or not someone is part of a religious institution, they are legitimate in the eyes of the universe if their inner child remains pure. That's what the universe observes – all positivity from us. Virtue is the common target for every soul navigating this world before returning to the radiant consciousness.

The Holy Bible is a Hebrew book that captures their history and worldview. It is fundamentally Jewish and represents their perspective on divinity and how the world functions. Recognizing this can help release other cultures and belief systems from claims of exclusive authority. The result would be a more harmonious world, with improved relationships and a brighter, more positive future.

Everyone's reality reflects their internal state – their attitude, aura, and actions are received by the universe and mirrored back in various ways. Everyone holds a belief system – their reality, what they project, and what's reflected back to them.

The Holy Bible is not the supreme oracle. There exists a higher law that surpasses the Christian Bible. Universalism is the original, timeless truth that pervades all humanity and cultures. The existence of universal truth explains the variety of pious doctrines worldwide.

<u>To repeat:</u> Christianity is not the only reality. It's just one aspect of the world's diverse faiths. All belief systems are valid for their originating cultures. Each reflects what society's seers promoted and has thus become their collective realism. The most important point is that any belief nurtures the Pure Spirit. It's less about religious rituals and more about maintaining a pure and healthy human spirit in daily life.

To expand, it's not about sects or denominations but about discovering a higher, pure self. We all emerge from the Universal Consciousness, born into this world with an untainted spirit. People, regardless of religious affiliation, are valid in life and death if their inner child remains uncorrupted. That's what the universe observes – all is positive for us.

Virtue is the universal goal for every soul journeying through life before returning to the luminous consciousness.

Vice opposes virtue. Those involved in vice do so because one or more chakras are unbalanced and lacking positive energy. This relates to chakra and aura health. While this should be recognized, it's often overlooked, especially in Western cultures influenced by JCO, which quotes sacred texts and attributes vice to sin and immorality. This standpoint misses the mark, trapping adherents in fear, guilt, and shame about their addictive behaviors.

This trauma further affects the aura, causing inner chakras to close and the inner child to feel insecure, inadequate, and punished. Such conditions hinder health and well-being, yet many remain trapped in this cycle. JCO does much good in the world, but a flawed foundation can lead to unproductive outcomes, causing suffering.

Moreover, it's egotistical for JCO to impose its beliefs on others of different faiths. Honest sincerity can lead to attempts at conversion, but often it's misguided when it conflicts with the other person's natural life phase or Peak Year for transformation. Many religious workers push for immediate conversions, disregarding the natural cosmic flow governed by Numbers. JCO often shows little respect for this divine flow, which is evident in its forceful interactions.

The Holy Bible is not the end of all. There is a higher law operating that dwarfs the Bible. The Bible has been adapted to suit the people of its time. This explains why there are many interpretations and varied beliefs among men of the sects. To conclude, let us remember the UNI principle: that this is one's perceived reality emanating from, and then reflected back, enforcing the personal interpretation.

Earth Bound or Other-Worldly

In UNI, the Base Chakra is about feeling connected to this planet and is healthy when one feels settled in life. JCO does not support this, but from its textbook to its sermons promotes detachment from this world. JCO fosters otherworldliness. 'A pilgrim was I and a wandering' is the mantra. 'This world is not my home; I'm just passing through' is another line.

This philosophy is problematic for the Base Chakra and can cause disturbances in the other energy centres, which may lead to emotional outbursts.

JCO fosters complexes in its patriotic members – such as the 'victim complex,' the 'martyr complex,' and 'the world is against me complex.' These long-term mental states can disrupt the balance of the chakras and make a person overly sensitive and reactive toward life's events and others.

In contrast, UNI aims to maintain chakra balance, leading to peace and harmony with life's events and others. It is about the health of the chakras, not about sin or violating any religious creed.

Generally speaking, fanatical adherents in fundamental and cultist institutions distrust the State, the internet, and social media. It is because of this 'the world is against me' mentality. An offshoot of extreme brainwashing is this 'Big Brother is trying to trap me' mindset.

To the person with typical thinking, this mindset is unsettling. Most people in the population have no issue with the internet and are more mentally relaxed. Most people feel more comfortable with themselves; accepting others and things outside of themselves more openly.

JCO promotes the concept of J.O.Y. – Jesus, Others, You. This again leans toward manipulation, as church members are conditioned to look to some ministerial figure. Although many find joy in helping others and putting themselves last, that can lead to imbalance and burnout. This has ruined many zealous lives. In the realm of prayer, one is taught that it is sinful to selfishly ask for things for oneself.

UNI promotes Y.O. – You, Others.

UNI holds a healthier perspective because we need to first understand and love ourselves before we can reach out to others. We must start by being at peace with our inner child, our higher self, balanced and in harmony. Then, relationships naturally flow from that sense of serenity. In the realm of prayer (or expressing affirmations to the universe), one should first ask for oneself to achieve balance and harmony, and then relationship needs will follow from that serenity. If this were widely understood, the world would be a much more liveable place. Harmony in relationships would usher in a new era, and positivity could flourish in a brighter future.

JCO advises people to ignore intuition. JCO teaches that intuition cannot be trusted. Followers are conditioned to distrust their personal clairvoyance. This guidance causes a disruption in the personal energy field. It's crucial to stay centred in self-love and trust to fully harness intuition.

Intuition originates from the Higher Self and should be embraced. It represents the true you connected to the universe and benevolent spirit guides. The Higher Self existed before entering this world and will persist after leaving. Within you lie all the answers to life's questions, divine essence, and necessary salvation. The journey involves discovering, loving, and trusting yourself. This promotes healthy chakras and the highest form of 'nirvana.'

JCO diverts people from this inner truth, causing them to seek outside themselves for discovery, love, and trust, thereby distorting the original divine purpose. People are conditioned to seek answers, divine essence, and salvation from others, completely missing the point.

Measuring up to the Standard

In JCO, one often feels inadequate. The textbook suggests that we never truly measure up. The Bible states that everyone begins from a very flawed starting point. From the doctrine of original sin to the doctrine of eternal damnation, we are in a difficult position before we even begin the journey.

In sermon material, there's always an expectation to be more, do more, give more, strive more, and work more, with harsh consequences for failure. There are only two options: try harder and risk failure, or give up and leave the church. As a result, many of JCO's converts backslide, burn out, and leave. This is a tragedy because people get hurt in the process, sometimes severely. Some remain unaware, but others see through the manipulative strategy of this system that constantly urges them to do more and give more.

In direct contrast, UNI assures us that the higher self has already been reached, and this life journey is about going inward to embrace this higher being. We have a small voice that guides us, and we are to follow it moment by moment. The higher self is a divine spark of the eternal universal fire that burns for our well-being (not harm). This means rest for the weary and light attire for our marathon walk.

If one departs from JCO, vice is not the only alternative left. Vice is something none of us should engage in because it causes hurt and shame to ourselves, our family, and our friends. There is another alternative to JCO – one that we should all choose: it is UNIVERSALISM and maintaining virtue and integrity.

It is the pure spirit within that is the key to every divine lock and the answer to every philosophical question. Everyone born into the world has this purity initially, and it is this that the Universe observes during and after one's earthly journey to determine lessons learned and those still to be acquired.

In JCO, the church family is wonderful and loving, but the underlying expectation to be perfect and above reproach causes deep insecurities that affect the health of the chakras. Beneath the layer of love, there is a bed of nails. When someone misses church meetings, they are considered a 'back-slider,' and when they leave the fold, they are regarded as a heathen. This is JCO's mistaken mindset and poor attitude toward fellow human beings who, at the very least, deserve basic respect. Nevertheless, we should not get too upset about all the harm others may do to us – after all, this is all but a dream.

UNI upholds the dignity of all human beings to find their own way without coercion or mistreatment. We each go through different seasons and cycles. One decade, we may focus on a particular theme, and the next, we might ignore that goal to focus on something new. This is natural, and we should accept that life consists of a series of experiences, lessons, and achievements. For example, the author's life is divided into three sets of eighteen years: the first centred on Family, the second on the Church, and the third on the Arts. Today, thanks to the 'gnostic' awareness I enjoy, I am completely at peace with having set aside the church to pursue my arts.

JCO, on the other hand, does not teach this nor allow such relinquishing of church attendance, fearing it might weaken their control over simple-minded individuals, reduce financial offerings, and damage their reputation with the hierarchical missionary board. It is common for believers to feel the urge to explore new interests in their aura, and so, in their programmed reality, they tell the bishop and elders that they believe it is God's will to move on. The clergy then compare this to the Bible and respond with objections to the idea. Since it does not align with the Bible, they claim it is not God's will. This can harm people, who then sit back down in the rear pew and deny the truth of their chakras. These individuals are harmed and led astray from their true divine path by people of the cloth.

There is no will from an external God, no biblically described Holy Spirit, and no negative reputation for crossing scripture. Instead, there is the Moon, which influences our mood, our 'tides,' and our cycles.

JCO has been responsible for causing harm in the world of men, from terrible crimes of war and bloodshed to the oppression of citizens who are denied their true destiny. People are prevented from pursuing their chakra dreams and finding direction in life, and as a result, they lose their way, especially since their high priest constantly claims to hold the only right path for them.

Absolutism and Relativism

In this universal experience that we all share, JCO is supposed to exist – there must be a reason why. It is up to each individual to decide how to live within or outside its framework, as the case may be – at the end of the day, that is what matters. Some JCO ministers of religion stir devotees to passion and fanaticism, leading to pushy converters of others.

Other institutions are more liberal and easy-going. In my opinion, the latter is more ideal than the former. "Live and let live" is the ancient mantra of the East – this promotes harmony, a loving testimony, and a peaceful lifestyle. All belief systems share common principles, such as loving one another and doing to others as one would have others do for them.

Some people have a mindset of absolutism, seeing themselves as conservative, radical, strict, and dogmatic in their views. Their worldview is received by the universe and reflected back to them. In a sense, they create their own reality. This reality, whether perceived as good or bad (with bumps in life's highway), results from their limiting and sometimes negative outlook. If someone perceives the world as against them, this perception is reinforced when negative events happen. This 'victim/martyr at war with the world' mentality is common in hardcore fundamental movements.

Some people have a mindset of liberalism, relativism, and are easy-going. Their worldview is also received by the universe and reflected back to them. In a sense, they create their own reality. The more positive their mindset, the better the reflection back into their lives, and the generous cycle continues.

All religions and sects around the world are different paths leading to the same goal. They all have the potential to guide to the same nirvana if respected as channels for the untainted spirit. Yes, we know that abuse of these systems sometimes occurs globally, but this does not negate the truth of the statement above. It is the purity of spirit that matters to the Universal Consciousness. Some people won't enter a church, let alone become members, yet they have a pure spirit—they are in harmony with the Universe.

Here is more: God is within, not without. You create your own reality. What you surround yourself with and give out comes back to you, shaping your reality.

Everyone's perception is their reality and a reflection of themselves: creating individual points of view. This explains why there are varied beliefs, interpretations, and perspectives. Additionally, the star sign one is born under and its specific implications for temperament contribute to even more variability among Homo sapiens on this planet.

A negative mindset attracts illness and more suffering into a person's life, while a positive attitude promotes health and well-being. Science and biology agree, showing that negative and positive states of mind trigger certain chemical processes in the body, which then lead to either gloom or vitality.

Health of Chakras

———

Limiting belief systems can cause some people to fall into sickness and ailments, which can result in the long-term suppression of personal potential and lead to serious health issues. When inspiration is blocked by a human-made code of rules involving severe threats of punishment for non-compliance, a subconscious fear affects the nervous and immune systems, leading to dis-ease.

Furthermore, the story is not about sin and wickedness. There is no place for discussions of sin. Instead, morals and ethics are valuable tools to maintain order in relationships. There is a universally accepted belief about what constitutes appropriate or inappropriate behaviour. For JCO to add sin, prejudice, and condemnation to the mix is unhelpful to human existence and cohesion. This is evident from the unrest, terrorism, wars, and disturbances that constantly afflict our species. When someone lives in a mental straitjacket of 'thou shalt not's, the internal energy becomes diminished, restricted, and unbalanced. This long-term condition leads to dis-ease.

I emphasize that it's not about sin, but rather about the health of the Chakras.

Chakras (meaning wheels) are seven major energy centres along the mid-line of the body, reflecting health and spiritual well-being. These Chakras function like multi-dimensional gateways, allowing individuals to access different experiences and levels of consciousness. Stress in various areas of life can cause energy blockages in specific chakras, leading to imbalance and dis-ease. You can clear these blockages through stretching, massage, meditation, color visualization, sound therapy, and spending time in nature. The chakras are constantly targeted by life experiences, which can cause imbalances and interruptions in energy flow. Everyone experiences stress in different parts of their body and mind. Our strengths and weaknesses are unique to each person. Each main vortex corresponds to particular functions and reflects our state of being. Learning about the chakras can help us develop effective strategies for healing ourselves.

Seven Main Chakras

<u>B</u>ase Chakra: root, located at the base of the spine. It is concerned with security, survival, and being settled and safe. The base chakra is associated with connection to the natural world.

<u>Colour:</u> Bright Red.

<u>Imbalance:</u> If this chakra is filled with fear, insecurity, anxiety, and instability, it can lead to dis-ease in the body from the hips down to the feet. Remember that the body is a holistic organism, where one part can affect another, so tension in the hip may also travel up the spinal muscles to the shoulders, neck, and skull, causing pain in these areas as well. An imbalance in the adrenal glands may result in a lack of energy and enthusiasm for life.

Sacral Chakra: It is in the sacral and lower lumbar area, concerned with bodily issues, reproduction, sensuality, and basic instincts.

<u>Colour:</u> Orange

<u>Imbalance:</u> insecure in sexual matters, suppression of natural needs and feelings. Possible ailments in the hip, lumbar, and sexual organs. The sacral plexus, testicles, and ovaries can be affected.

Solar Plexus Chakra: Located just above the navel, it is concerned with personal control and power, as well as inner calm and acceptance of others.

<u>Colour:</u> Golden Yellow

<u>Imbalance:</u> distrust of universal flow and a need to dominate (control freak). An emphasis on the material. There can be digestive, nervous, and circulatory system ailments.

<u>Heart Chakra</u>: Located in the chest, it is concerned with love and relationships, as well as tolerance and acceptance of oneself and others.

<u>Colour:</u> Green

<u>Imbalance:</u> insincere love and inability to receive love. There may be ailments affecting the thymus gland, cardiac plexus, heart, lungs, and shoulders.

<u>Throat Chakra</u>: Located in the throat area, it is concerned with communication and creativity.

<u>Colour:</u> Sky Blue

<u>Imbalance:</u> inability to express oneself; fear of being censored. There may be issues related to the thyroid, throat, and neck.

<u>Brow Chakra</u>: Located in the forehead, it is concerned with intuition and imagination.

<u>Colour:</u> Indigo Purple

<u>Imbalance:</u> rejection of spiritual/mystical aspects of life. There may be disturbances in the pineal gland (which controls cycles of rest and activity).

<u>Crown Chakra</u>: Located at the crown and is concerned with knowledge, understanding, and connection to the Universe.

<u>Colour:</u> Violet, White

<u>Imbalance:</u> disconnect from unity with the divine, depression, and dissatisfaction. There may be issues with the pituitary gland, endocrine system, and cerebral cortex.

The Universe is the higher Cosmic Mind (consciousness). Everything that happens in your life and reality is an expression of this Universal Mind. Your experiences are a dream of the Cosmic Mind.

You are at the center of your world. Open your eyes and look around. Everything is arranged around you in a circle or sphere. You are at the center. This is a key insight in the internal arts. The martial art of Aikido is based on this principle for both defense and attack.

<u>Note:</u>

- The lower two chakras (Root and Sacral) represent our physical body and the physical world.

- The middle three chakras (Solar, Heart, and Throat) govern our control, emotions, and communication.

- The upper two chakras (Brow and Crown) relate to our intuition, clairvoyance, and connection to the Universe.

The middle plane is concerned with morals, immorality, good and bad, and the distinction between naughty and nice. The middle chakras are about moral and social issues.

The top plane is the spiritual plane and is about connection to the spiritual realm. To be one with the universal force is to be in the ideal experience. There is no moral concern in this arena. There is no cause to be afraid of the higher power. Perfect love casts out fear.

Sent Out and Reflected Back

Unlock the Mysteries of Existence with "The Chi Key"! Are you troubled by the shadows of uncertainty? Do the mysteries of the cosmos leave you perplexed? Fear not! Within these pages lies a revelation—a beacon of light to guide you through the cosmic labyrinth.

I am about to give you the powerful key that unlocks you, others, the world, and the universe. Many sages and wise men have searched for this; many philosophers have lived and died missing it. Are you ready for it? THE CHI KEY is this: everything in the Universe operates on NUMBERS and VIBRATIONS. This publication explores this Key. Keep an open mind, and the light will illuminate.

Everyone's reality reflects who they are: what is inside them (attitude), their aura (around them), and their actions (coming out of them) are received by the Universe and reflected back in different ways. Everyone has a belief system: that is their reality—what they send out and what gets reflected back to them.

The CHI KEY encompasses this idea that what is within a person, permeates their aura, and then emerges, is received by Universal Consciousness and mirrored back. The timing of this reflection is controlled by NUMBERS, and the strength of it is measured by VIBRATIONS.

The Universe uses numbers and vibrations. Numbers determine when someone is born, when life stages start and end, the timing of death, and rebirth. Everything is mapped out for you at every stage of your journey. Nothing is left to chance or surprises the higher self. This awareness frees the inner child to fulfill its destiny and brightens the auric rainbow that cloaks the physical body. Accepting this 'gnostic' knowledge is like graduating into adulthood on the way to nirvana.

How people think, live, and treat each other is what is received by the Universe and reflected back.

Enlightenment after the Dark Room

In this celestial compendium, I reveal THE CHI KEY—a treasure built through years of exploration, sacrifice, and discovery. Now, dear seeker, I present it to you at a small part of its cosmic value.

<u>Your Inner Mechanism:</u> Discover how you tick, pulse, and resonate. Peel back the layers of your soul and witness the symphony within.

<u>The Human Tapestry:</u> Understand how others dance to their cosmic rhythms. Decode their essence, their fears, and their hopes.

<u>The Cosmic Choreography:</u> Behold the grand ballet of stars, planets, and nebulae. You are a note in this cosmic symphony.

The CHI KEY reveals that what is within a person permeates their aura, and what emerges is received by the Universal Consciousness and reflected back. The timing of this process is governed by NUMBERS, and its force is measured by VIBRATIONS.

<u>To repeat:</u> the Universe uses numbers and vibrations. Numbers determine when you are born, when life stages start and end, the timing of death, and rebirth. Everything is mapped out for you at every moment of your journey; nothing is left to chance or surprise to the higher self.

Compare this to the darkened 'college classrooms' of JCO, with all its sincerity and well-meaning gestures; it falls short of delivering what is promised, yet it constantly lectures students on 'examination passes and fails.'

The investigation into Numerology and Horoscope fields pays rich dividends to the seeker of truth when one understands that life is governed by number patterns.

In the Horoscope, there are twelve zodiac signs, and each sign is ruled by a governing planet along with lesser planets that influence it. These planets emit vibrations that stimulate or diminish the traits of those born during that period. These vibrational effects are similar to how the moon influences the vast oceans of Earth. Every celestial planet that moves through your twelve houses each day, week, month, and year affects how you feel when you wake up and the events that unfold throughout your day.

This main grouping of twelve star-sign personality types provides reassurance and clarity about how people function, relate to others, and the overview of their life journey and ultimate destiny. It not only explains why there are differences in characteristics among individuals but also confirms that each life is built on a solid foundation and that there is a key lesson to learn throughout this journey. Compared to the chaotic confusion of JCO, which claims that a superior being controls your life—sometimes benevolent, sometimes antagonistic, depending on your attitude and religious practices—this perspective offers clarity. It's like a song about Santa Claus watching to see if you are naughty or nice. If a tragic event such as an overwhelming loss occurs, clergy may tell you it is God's will and that you should blindly trust the situation to God. However, rational minds realize that they cannot receive a clear explanation from the clergy why this happened, which leaves them feeling stuck.

Sickness and Prayer

Sickness reflects what is happening inside an individual. When a person is restrained in communication, the throat chakra becomes unbalanced. Hip problems indicate that the root chakra is out of alignment, leading to difficulty feeling settled and safe in life. Leg and knee issues relate to mobility, possibly signalling a feeling of being stuck in a life rut. This is why UNI says illness is not about sin but about the health of the chakras. When someone is trapped in an addiction, JCO states they are a BAD person. UNI clarifies they are a SICK person. It's all about the health of the chakras and the aura energy field.

On a larger scale, this explains why some nations face severe poverty and famine while others are wealthy. It reflects the collective political, cultural, and religious mindset of a nation.

Prayers are one's desires sent out into space. JCO believes that these prayers are received by the one God, as described in their textbook. This divine personality may or may not answer their prayer requests.

UNI adherents pin a list of affirmative statements on the wall and read these out in passing. Some may have a dream board where affirmations and images are fastened to tell their subconscious where they wish to be in the future. These requests sent out to the Universal Consciousness fulfil the exact same purpose as religious prayers. Even though the actions and perceptions may differ slightly, they are of the same essence. There is no group higher than another or one sect more privileged than another. All humankind is on level ground to send out their wishes and be heard.

The question of why some requests are answered, and others are not, can be explained by UNI, as what we receive is first a reflection of what is within us, around us, and emanating from us. If someone has a pure spirit and is in harmony with the universal flow, positivity is returned to them repeatedly. The timing of events, including delays, relates to numbers and planetary alignments in our star sign zone.

If we maintain a positive mindset and persevere with our honest desires, we can expect solutions and dreams to come true at the right time.

It is not about appeasing a deity to get prayers answered, as jungle natives or people of the cloth often try to do. It is not about offering bloody sacrifices or attending every church meeting to satisfy a supreme being. We are the deity. YOU are the deity. Recognizing this marks the transition from the school of JCO to the adult life of UNI. JCO religion represents the immature stage of the cocoon where one relies on a prop. UNI is the butterfly stage, bringing enlightenment and a new sense of inner peace. This aspect of the CHI KEY offers freedom and protection from manipulative systems. If you are God and part of the divine whole, then you define your own story, your own journey, and your own path. Because you love, honor, and believe in yourself, you hold the power to accept or reject religious and relationship pressures and peer influences.

<u>To reiterate:</u> in graduation, peace resides in the soul, and as global awareness grows, peace reaches around the world. There is a rising global focus on cultivating positivity through meditation for a new era of harmony. Eastern philosophies practice universal meditation techniques, and this influence has been spreading worldwide, especially since the 1960s in the West, to promote positive change.

Although JCO has made notable contributions to humanitarian efforts, it has also historically caused division, prejudice, and harm through its limited and restrictive programming. It has been said before that the absence of fundamental JCO and the awareness of UNI could lead to a period of peace worldwide.

When JCO members pray, they consider the idea of an intelligent God, a higher being, as described in the Holy Bible. JCO claims that a holy God only listens to his righteous followers. The issue with this view is that miracles occur worldwide and happen to the unchurched as well – they have prayers answered along with warm feelings.

Even though the conditioned mind thinks about one superior being, the reality is that people are praying to spirit guides who make their presence felt through warm, reassuring motions. These friendly spirits, floating around the atmosphere, look out for our interests and work behind the scenes to bring answers to our wishes. These ex-humans help guide us, boost our belief, and reassure us that what we have asked for is on the way.

Once again, prayer answers depend on what has been sent out into the cosmos—a reflection returned in the form of miracles. Prayer outcomes are influenced by variables within the spiritual and social realms: what is happening in the larger context of the situation and how people are affected. These questions reverberate through the ether as people wait for answers. This explains why some prayers are answered and others are not, and why, across the globe, regardless of belief systems, people experience different levels of success with prayer. When the guides withdraw their attention temporarily, it creates a feeling of a wall of silence, contrasting with the warm assurance of communication.

The Afterlife

There is positivity in life and after physical death. There is no Hell, biblically described or otherwise.

There is no Triune God as described in the Holy Bible. However, there are Spirit Guides in the Universe and in the world around the living. These spirits are benevolent former humans who are in a period of settling any unfinished business related to their past lives before moving into the white light of the Universe to fully reconnect with The Consciousness, until their number lines up again for rebirth onto the earth. Let us look at a few possible instances:

1: <u>Terminal illness or sudden accidental death</u> – unfinished business keeps these spirits hovering over loved ones and affairs until they feel everything is going to be fine. Depending on the psychic abilities of the living, these bereaved ghosts may try to communicate with loved ones to close family affairs (either directly or through a medium). Depending on their frustration level, the energies in their old home may become disrupted. Remember, they seek resolution so they can float off to their Nirvana.

2: <u>Brutal, Murderous, and Aggrieved Death</u> – These ghosts are enraged over the injustice of their lives being cut short and cannot rest until justice is served. They may disturb the energies at their site of grievance. This paranormal activity is commonly reported as spirits haunting a house or location. It is the sort of thing horror books and movies depict.

These are two examples that effectively illustrate paranormal activity in the world of the living.

Not all spirits linger, though: only those who need to settle unfinished business. The others leave their physical shells, enter the white light, and float off to their Nirvana.

This understanding explains a lot, not just about paranormal activity but also about prophets, seers, and gurus who claim psychic experiences such as inspiration, visions, and foreknowledge from the ethereal realm.

In JCO, the text states that the Holy Spirit is responsible for anointing holy saints to record the content of scripture.

Instead, let me suggest that this is simply what the ancestors assigned supernatural experiences to in their time.

In human interactions, Spirit Guides (specializing in religion) influence susceptible people to dedicate themselves to a role, using whatever means necessary to guide the subject according to their template.

There have been prophets throughout history and in the present day. Prophets are enlightened and led by their Spirit Guide to perform supernatural feats. Prophets spend time in passive meditative sessions and are attuned to the spirit world.

However, not every spirit is benevolent or looking to the betterment of the living. For instance, anyone who claims to hear voices speaking in their head, telling them to commit a malicious act, has fallen prey. Such a victim is telling it as they see it or hear it, as the case may be. A spirit has gained a foothold in their life and possesses their aura for ill-disciplined ends.

There is no biblically described angelic being called the Devil, Lucifer, or Satan; instead, these are creations of Judaism and Christianity used to explain to children in dark bedrooms why things go bump in the night. At some point, it became popular to label spooky and mischievous phenomena as being caused by an angelic being—Satan.

The ancient civilizations of the UNI believed that the planet Saturn was the source of all mischief, obstacles, troubles, delays, disappointments, illnesses, and frustrations. All planets have meanings, and their vibrations have a direct influence on life on Earth. Saturn's vibrations hinder progress, reduce returns, drain energy, weaken health, and restrict freedom.

When Judaism recounted its national history, it attributed a series of unfortunate events to a fallen angel, shifting the understanding from planetary influence to demonic influence. Christianity adopted this changed belief, which has allowed it to instill great fear into the hearts of billions of 'lost' people over the centuries.

The editors of sacred texts used this idea to instill fear in impressionable people. Fearful individuals programmed to rely on the priesthood for protection are much easier to control than a group of freethinkers. UNI states that it is the planet Saturn that generates these negative vibrations in a person's life, along with numbers that influence the timing of unfortunate events. Such a realization does not produce fear but leads to understanding, acceptance, and the ability to cope. Understanding the planet's vibrational influence explains why bad things happen to good people and why rain falls on both the just and the unjust. Vibrations emanate and reach us all, regardless of moral strength. There is one small caveat: the pure, dutiful, and sacrificial may prevail over harmful impacts, while the adulterated and weak may struggle.

Higher Consciousness

Biblical characters, historical stories, and experiences are undoubtedly valid, but the Bible story is a Jewish story focusing on belief in one supreme being – Jehovah.

As we have stated with all courtesy, there is no one superior being; instead, we have departed souls who spirit around the ether, guarding, guiding, and governing.

Throughout history, we see that from time to time, the universe gives birth to anointed individuals, and guardian angels are assigned to care for them. These chosen ones receive special attention. They exhibit increased activity and power when tuned into their higher consciousness. This explains the lives of prophets and apostles, as well as countless individuals across global history, religious traditions, and modern life. Miracle workers, divine healers, clairvoyants, diviners, mediums, monks, magicians, and mystics are illuminated for special work between dimensions.

Miracle workers can be found in every faith and in the vast auditorium as well as the animalistic jungle. It doesn't matter what the dogma is. No sect has a monopoly on miracles and healing.

Anyone tuned into their higher consciousness vibrates at a higher level, tapping into the universal truth, provision, and power.

The higher vibrating aura has the color of violet/white. Such a person has no negative etheric ties. A person vibrating at a high level easily connects to the spiritual realm.

Spirit Guides Along the Way

No biblical Hades or Gehenna awaits the lost soul. There is hope after physical death. When one leaves the fleshly body, they may linger for a while to resolve unfinished business or pass through the white light tunnel of an alternate dimension. One might stay in interplanetary heaven for earthly decades, waiting for their turn to be reborn into a different family and country.

There are spirit guides who stay here to help people reach their full potential. These guides have gone through life cycles before and have experience with the journey. Depending on how receptive living individuals are, these guides have different levels of influence: the more open they are, the more help spirits can provide.

Regarding the author's story, I have long worked with guidance from above. In my Christian philosophy, I believed these were the workings of God and the Holy Spirit, but now I realize they were the actions of spirit guides who communicated with my inner self and helped me along the way, hearing my sincere prayers and orchestrating all things through numbers and vibrations.

The existence of spirit guides could also explain events of a mystical nature: visions, impressions, visitations, and flashes of insight; not only in my ministry experience but also in others' experiences throughout history. For example, the founding of religions, sects, and cults can all be linked to sacred visitations. From Emperor Constantine to Joan of Arc, from Joseph Smith to Ellen White, and from Mohammed to Martin Luther, mystical experiences from beyond have played a crucial role in the origins of religious movements, reformations, and revivals.

Here is a list of activities that Spirit Guides do for us:

- Guides are concerned with all aspects of our daily lives, even small things like the car not starting when we're late for work.

- Guides are aware of every part of our lives and know us better than we know ourselves, with perfect knowledge and clear perception of our social circle, work struggles, and hobby goals.

- Guides are proud of where we have come from and what we have accomplished so far.

- Guides encourage us to live in the present: accept what is, let go of what was, and believe in what will be.

- Guides remind us that our power resides within each of us and that this power is only realized today. Everything is always working out for us.

- Guides, as former humans, are specialists in various fields and connect with us to assist in our chosen pursuits. These fields include religion, sports, construction, creative arts, music composition, wellness, agriculture, and others.

- Guides promote you as the top priority. Everything revolves around you.

- Guides are here to help you fulfill your true life ambitions.

My Personal Story – Reflection

The CHI KEY contains this gem – everyone's reality is a reflection of themselves: what is in them (attitude), around them (aura), and coming out of them (actions) is received by the Universe and reflected back in various ways. Everyone has a belief system – that is their reality. This reality is sent out and reflected back to them.

As the author, I want to reflect on my own journey so far. During my first eighteen years on the farm, I was a natural man. In the following eighteen years with the Church, I became a soul man. In the last eighteen years, I have grown into a spiritual man.

In my own story, I was raised in a nominal Christian home, and I sought to know God. This is what I sent out to the Universe, and a deep personal awareness of the spiritual realm was reflected back to me. I was open, and therefore I experienced mystical moments. I asked in prayer for an adventurous Christian life, and guess what – that is what I received. (That story is told in the autobiography: Memoir of a Pilgrim Preacher).

While I was in the church period, I was financially poor because the JCO programming claimed that poverty was a sign of piety. The church was happy to accept my money, and the offering bag was bottomless. I believed this and spoke it, and it became my reality. Today, that biblical belief is cast off like an old coat, and I think wealth. I believe in rich ideas, and wealth is now my reality.

During my eighteen years in the church, I became quite focused, as one does in a fundamental system. I was a passionate advocate for God and the truth. From a sincere heart, I shared God's message through personal testimony and preaching.

Near the end of those years, karma caught up with me, and I went through a dark two-year period, during which certain people judged me harshly and diminished my personal power. My two years of depression led up to a peak period for me. I was powerless to escape the trial until the Numbers came up, and I was released into the new life of UNI.

Now, on the other side, and in the light of UNI enlightenment, I realize that the universe has caused me to reap what I had previously sown in the lives of others. However, the universe understood that I carried out all things sincerely, and so it measured the incoming vibrations mercifully. In the third set of eighteen years, I was free to focus on my art. I have also received guidance in the fields of health and well-being.

What is life about? Are you ready for the answer? It is about virtue, being true to yourself, and enjoying life. That's what it ultimately comes down to. I write this universal truth in the hope that it will open the eyes of religious believers and help them break free from human-made rules and regulations. I also write for the un-churched, to say, this is the way—walk in it.

- <u>Virtue</u> encompasses wholesomeness, self-love, and self-belief.

- <u>Being yourself</u> is about who the Universe influences one to be and do in life.

- <u>Having a good time</u> in life means appreciation, positivity, responsibility, and fun.

<u>In life, there are two dire paths to avoid</u>:

- <u>Recklessness:</u> self-destructive habits and harmful actions. Self-sabotage.

- <u>Restrictive belief systems:</u> religious, social, or political codes that restrict one's freedom, deter from one's life path, and ultimately cause harm.

The author was deeply involved in conservative Christianity for twenty years, and the programming and peer pressure prevented me from pursuing the internal arts, saving my money, accepting all people, and enjoying popular activities.

Although the JCO way promoted virtue and kept me from going down harmful paths, it also stopped me from following my heart in some important parts of life.

The reader might have a similar story to share about their experiences.

THE CHI KEY UNLOCKS:

<u>Peace Amidst Chaos:</u> Every challenge becomes a stepping stone. Life's stages unfold with grace.

<u>Afterlife Assurance:</u> Fear not the great beyond. The Chi Key whispers of continuity, of cosmic reunion.

<u>Freedom from Belief Shackles:</u> Break free from dogmas. Embrace the boundless truth that transcends creeds.

<u>Escape the Emotional Undertow:</u> Negative cycles dissipate. Your mind becomes a crystal-clear pool of understanding.

<u>Relationship Alchemy:</u> Decode hearts, mend bonds. See the constellations in their eyes.

<u>Self-Love's Genesis:</u> The Chi Key ignites the spark within. Transform, evolve, love unconditionally.

<u>Intuitive Alignment:</u> Truth resonates. Your intuition becomes a compass in the cosmic wilderness.

Global Numerology

The global world also functions on numbers and experiences Peak Years. These are periods of significant upheaval and change when Peak Years come into play. They represent times of major reform among humanity. For example, the ministry of Jesus of Nazareth in Palestine, during which his faction originated and disrupted the region, would be one such peak period in world history. This was a time of upheaval for ritualistic Judaism and the rise of the Christian sect, where people sought enlightenment and a champion for the oppressed.

Prevalent worldviews are also projected out, received by the Universe, and reflected back to shape the situations we observe, whether as our history or current events; whether as global incidents or local news. There are Peak Years for specific countries, regions, cities, towns, villages, families, and individuals. This explains, for example, why countries experience boom-and-bust cycles, civil wars and peace periods, corruption, and religious revivals.

Additionally, there are Peak Years for various industries such as agriculture, technology, construction, wellness, manufacturing, education, political and civil sectors, emergency services, enforcement, defense, and commerce.

Furthermore, the world has been moving over millennia through the 'Zodiac,' with each sign carrying specific meanings and influences affecting the planet and all living beings. For instance, in recent centuries, humanity has experienced rapid technological advances, aligning with the Zodiac scale's timeline for that period. Currently, the Zodiac scale indicates a phase of global enlightenment among humans, a period that likely began in the 1960s and has gained momentum since.

Moreover, each Chakra symbolizes a stage in the evolution of this planet and its life forms. From the Base Chakra, representing the survival of the human race—similar to the cavemen era—to the Crown Chakra, symbolizing global enlightenment, we see this progression reflected throughout human history.

These various fields of Universalism are discussed in this book. They offer avenues for the reader to explore further, and such study can bring great rewards. JCO doesn't and won't inform you about these fields of Universalism, for the reasons explained in this book. In short, the Bible textbook fosters fear among both clergy and laity, causing other serious issues like shame and guilt. Understand that controlling the population is the balancing act of both politics and JCO religion.

In contrast, UNI fosters free thinkers who are attuned to their own psychic abilities, able to express themselves, and pursue their dreams. JCO and UNI have opposing goals.

Global graduation from the schoolhouse of JCO signifies that people will inherit peace in their souls. As global awareness grows, so does peace in the world. There is a rising focus among people of the new age on meditating positivity into creation for a new era of harmony. Eastern philosophies practice universal meditation techniques, and this influence has been spreading worldwide, especially since the 1960s in the West, to promote positive change.

Although JCO has brought about many humanitarian benefits, it has also historically caused division, prejudice, and harm through its limited and restrictive programming. JCO has been associated with turmoil, martyrs, terrorists, fanatics, and judgmental individuals. It has been said before that the diminishing of fundamental JCO, along with the increasing global awareness of UNI, would lead to a reign of peace in the world.

Energy Inter-Play

Regarding auric energy - it's not just that energy flows through us, but that we are the energy. We are a ball of fire. No energy is entirely and permanently negative or positive – energy, like fire, is constantly changing and exchanging.

The main influence of change comes from the vibrational energies of the planets in their orbit. Each planet affects us over a period of time, sometimes bringing us good blessings and other times poor luck. Sometimes, it influences our mood to be passive or aggressive. (This is a study in itself).

So, when there is dissent within a group, it is not about the people themselves: it's about the energy dynamics. It helps to focus on this during times of hardship or conflict. It's not the people (whom we see and sense), but rather, the underlying energy at play.

The energy in a human isn't permanently dark or light but shifts due to planetary alignments, casting shadows and then sunlight. Each person has auric energy that is variably influenced by the planets, which affects their tempers and smiles.

You know that one person you meet may repel you while another may attract you. You get along well with some and dislike others. It's about energy interplay. It's often called magnetism. Energy in auric personalities is active. Vibrations emanate and interact.

Some star signs are antagonistic toward your star sign. Your sign will encounter other signs that are not suitable for a long-term, meaningful relationship. This means you will be repelled by some signs, and certain people might get on your nerves. It's best to avoid partnering with some signs, no matter how appealing they seem.

Some examples of signs that are incompatible for long-term relationships are Aries with Cancer, Taurus with Aquarius, Gemini with Virgo, and Leo with Scorpio.

There are favourable signs akin to yours as well. These people will be attracted to you, and they make life fun. It is fine to couple up with these people. You can look online to see which signs are compatible with your sign.

<u>Each planet has a different meaning and influence upon this Earth and its inhabitants:</u>

- Mercury: speedy timing, communication

- Venus: love, romance, and bond

- Mars: war, conflicts, hardness

- Jupiter: attempting big things, big projects

- Neptune: dreaming and intuition

- Pluto: conclusion and re-birth

- Sun: you, inner personality

- Moon: moods and temperament

- Saturn: hindrances, frustration, and restrictions

This knowledge is illuminating and life-changing, as are all the deliberations in this book.

Peak Years and Valleys

The study of Numerology provides completely accurate, detailed insights into your life purpose. Valuing your life here, embracing your full potential, and having the ability to pursue future opportunities are the real good news.

In Numerology, you can calculate your Personal Year, also called the Peak Year, which rotates in nine-year cycles where major changes and new beginnings happen. The Peak Year is when one door closes and another major door opens.

The Peak Year is when energy concentrates and a new door opens, promising achievement. The eight years between Peak Years are the learning phase. Near the eighth year, you might feel stuck and crave change. Instead, use this newfound knowledge to embrace the valley, where important lessons are learned and growth occurs, preparing you for the upcoming Peak Year of transformation. You are here on earth to develop yourself, love yourself, understand your purpose, and use your gifts.

Your Life Path number is the age or year when you begin a nine-year cycle. You start your numerological journey at that specific age or year within your cycle.

For example, if your life path number (the sum of your birth date digits) is five, then that is the age when your nine-year cycle started. This cycle continues to rotate until the pilgrimage ends. Your Peak Year lasts from birthday to birthday, but be aware that intense energy can influence not only that year but also the period just before and after it. Like all cycles, there is a transition — valley years gradually rise to the peak and then fall into the valley of responsible engagement.

So, the peak period will introduce itself with unsettled energy lasting more than twelve months. Family may not understand you; friends could drift away, and your colleagues at work might challenge you. But you must persevere as you welcome these changing times! During a Peak Year, you might change careers, relocate, or switch partners. There may be a significant shift in perspective and beliefs. Something very important transforms. The old version of yourself is peeled away to make space for the new you.

This could mean a new location with a fresh circle of friends. It may also involve leaving your church group to embrace a better universal philosophy. Additionally, it might mean moving from renting to owning your own house.

Whatever happens, it is exciting, for your benefit, and supported by those in the unseen dimension.

Your Full Birth Name

There is power in using your full birth name. It helps align you with your inner child, which brings about strength, increased intuition, higher IQ, better peripheral vision, inner peace, self-love, and self-confidence.

As with the birth date numbers, the name that you use is permeated by vibrational energy, which affects your day and your destiny.

Using your full birth name unlocks your full potential. The numbers align when you include your middle name (if you have one) and avoid using a shortened version.

If you change your surname through marriage, it affects the name numbers and adds a new dimension to your life.

You can recalculate and see what the numbers mean.

<u>Coming Up! How to work out your Personal Numerology.</u>

Be proud of your birth name, believe in its purpose of being in existence, adopt it, and have fun visualizing what it will draw into your life.

If you need to change your name to utilize its full power, it may take a few months for the new name vibrations to produce positive results in the form of your heart's desires coming into your field of reality.

Numerology Basic Calculations

Here are the numerical calculations to determine your numbers. In this publication, I have not specified the contexts to explain the interpretations of the numbers. I invite you to obtain a book or visit a web page on Numerology to read the full story of what your numbers mean.

In Numerology, the five main calculations are the following:

<u>Birth Day</u> - represents your talents, skills, and how you relate to others daily.

<u>Life Path</u> - represents the direction of your life: challenges, experiences, and career.

<u>Soul Number</u> - represents your true character: drive, ambition, and heart's desire.

<u>Outer Personality</u> - represents how the world sees you: image and impression.

<u>Destiny Number</u> - represents what you came into life to accomplish: what you are good at.

The general rule when working out your numbers is to add all relevant numbers and then reduce the numbers to a single digit. Some say the exceptions to the rule are the Master Numbers - the double numbers 11, 22, and 33 - can be left as they are. Master numbers carry extra potency and are associated with angels and guides.

<u>Calculations</u>

Birth Day - represents your talents, skills, and how you relate to others daily. This is the day you were born. If you were born on a single-digit day, then that is your number. If you were born on a double-digit day, then add the digits together:

E.G. the 14th day. 1 + 4 = 5 The Number is **5**

Life Path - represents the direction of your life: challenges, experiences, and career. Add all the numbers of your birth date together, and then reduce to a single digit:

E.G. the 18th of March (third month of year) 1968

1 + 8 + 3 + 1 + 9 + 6 + 8 = 36 3 + 6 = **9** is the Life Path number.

Soul Number - represents your true character: drive, ambition, and heart's desire. To convert and calculate your full birth name is easy using the chart below.

Note: Any name change during life alters the dimension of your Soul Number and Outer Number. It is best to utilize the full power of your given birth name.

1 - A J S

2 - B K T

3 - C L U

4 - D M V

5 - E N W

6 - F O X

7 - G P Y

8 - H Q Z

9 - I R

Write down your full birth name and write the equivalent numbers for each <u>Vowel</u> above - this is to work out your Soul Number.

Then write down the equivalent numbers for each <u>Consonant</u> below. This is to work out your Outer Personality Number. This represents how the world sees you: image and impression.

Again, we add all the numbers in each line together and then reduce them to a single digit:

E.G. John Smith

6 9

J O H N S M I T H

1 8 5 1 4 2 8

<u>**Soul Number:**</u> $6 + 9 = 15$

$1 + 5 = \mathbf{6}$

<u>**Outer Personality Number:**</u> $1 + 8 + 5 + 1 + 4 + 2 + 8 = 29$

$2 + 9 = \mathbf{11} \; (= \mathbf{2})$

<u>**Destiny Number**</u> - represents what you came into life to accomplish: what you are good at. To work out this number, add all of the vowels and consonants of your birth name together, and reduce it to a single digit:

E.G. John Smith

$15 + 29 = 44$

$$4 + 4 = 8$$

These are the Numerical basic calculations to determine your personal numbers. In this publication, I have not given the story or context to explain the interpretation of the numbers. I invite you to obtain a book or a web page on Numerology to read the full story of what your numbers mean.

Numerology Potential Benefits

In this publication, I have not given the story or context to explain the interpretation of the numbers. I invite you to obtain a book or a web page on Numerology to read the full story of what your numbers mean. Utilize your numbers to find out where you have been, where you are now, and where you are expected to go.

Discover your purpose in life so that you can set exciting goals and pursue them with confidence!

Understand your experiences and challenges in daily life so that you can overcome all obstacles.

Find your career path: your ideal occupation, utilizing your natural talents, and enriching your life.

Understand what motivates you and others, enhancing your relationships.

Using a Numerology book or website with its readings for each calculated number, you can see how your house's street number influences your home life experiences.

Researching the subject further, you can work out your Temporary Numbers - these are the numbers that influence you day by day, week by week, month by month, and year by year.

Birth Chart

L et me add a brief point to this topic, which I will only touch on. The reader can explore this subject further on their own. The topic I am referring to is The Personal Birth Chart.

If you follow horoscope readings in your weekly media publication and are impressed with their general applications to your birth sign, then the Birth Chart offers a much deeper analysis of your personhood. The information in the birth chart is entirely personal and accurate for each individual. On the web, some sites can calculate your personal Birth Chart. All the calculator needs is your date of birth, time of birth, and place of birth. If you provide all these details, you will receive a printout with every detail about you, based on the planetary positions at the time of your birth.

In the circle, there are Twelve Houses. Each of these twelve houses represents a different perspective of our lives. They symbolize various themes and areas, including family, career, personal goals, fortune, romance and fun, health and fitness, social aspects, self-esteem, beliefs, aspirations, and more. The chart shows the positions of planetary bodies within these house segments. The placement of planets influences the traits associated with each house, shaping your life experiences. This means that certain parts of your life will be emphasized while others may recede, explaining why specific aspects of life change over time. The planetary positions in the Twelve Houses at the time and place of your birth indicate your initial setup for your journey here on Earth.

<u>They tell you:</u>

- about your make-up; the real you (Sun)

- your image that is shown to other people

- your fortune or lack of luck when reaching for goals (Jupiter)

- your inclinations to marriage, family, and having children

- What career you are best suited for

- your emotional state and level of confidence (moon)

- how romantic you are

And much more...

Each of the twelve Houses signifies a different area or theme of your life, such as family, career, personal goals, fortune, romance and fun, health and fitness, social life, self-esteem, view of the universe, and others. If a house in the circle has no planet in it (blank), it indicates that you have little or no interest in that aspect of your life. If a planet appears in a house but is in 'retrograde,' it suggests you may not make much progress in that area, experiencing a two steps forward and one step back situation.

It also matters which planet is in each house of your chart. Each planet has a different meaning and influence on this earth and its inhabitants.

- Mercury: speedy timing, communication

- Venus: love, romance and bond

- Mars: war, conflicts, hardness

- Jupiter: attempting big things; big projects

- Neptune: dreaming and intuition

- Pluto: conclusion and re-birth

- Sun: you, inner personality

- Moon: moods and temperament

- Saturn: hindrances, frustration, and restrictions

So, it will benefit the reader to personally explore this eye-opening subject further. This hidden information reveals who you are and what you are best suited to do during your time here on earth. And think about this: for each future soul rebirth on this planet, you get to come back for another opportunity in your next visit. Your soul will return on a different birth date with a new life-path number and different planetary alignments. For example, you may be reborn with the life-path number eight and be a practical money-maker; or return as a number nine, spending your days as a romantic dreamer, artistic and imaginative. This is both interesting and exciting!

The Principle of Universal Reflection

Let's summarize the concept of universal reflection and how the universe responds to our actions, both positive and negative. In this book, we have discussed the principle that what we emit into the world—whether it's kindness, negativity, or energy—ultimately reflects back to us.

The universe is an intricate web of interconnected energies, constantly in motion. From the tiniest subatomic particles to the grand cosmic structures, everything resonates with a subtle harmony. The principle of universal reflection posits that our thoughts, emotions, and deeds ripple through this cosmic fabric, affecting not only our immediate surroundings but also our own lives.

The Law of Reflection is also seen in an analogy from physics—the law of reflection. When light waves encounter a smooth surface, they bounce back at an angle equal to their angle of incidence. Similarly, our intentions and actions reverberate through the universe, returning to us in unexpected ways - whether we emit positivity or negativity, the cosmos mirrors our energy.

Sending Out Good Vibes: The Cosmic Echo

Kindness Multiplied: When we extend kindness, compassion, and love, the universe amplifies these vibrations. A smile shared with a stranger, a helping hand offered to someone in need—these acts resonate far beyond their immediate impact. They create a positive feedback loop, attracting more goodness into our lives.

Energy Flows: Just as a pebble dropped into a pond creates concentric ripples, our positive actions set off a chain reaction. The energy we release flows outward, touching lives we may never directly encounter. Perhaps our small act of generosity inspires someone else to pay it forward, creating a cascade of goodwill.

The Dark Side: Negative Reflections

<u>The Shadow Self:</u> Our negative emotions—anger, envy, resentment—also echo throughout the cosmos. When we harbor ill will or harm others, the universe registers these vibrations. The law of reflection doesn't discriminate; it reflects negativity just as efficiently as positivity.

<u>Karmic Debt:</u> Ancient philosophies speak of karma—the cosmic balance sheet. Every action accumulates a karmic debt or credit. If we harm others, that debt returns to haunt us. Conversely, acts of kindness build positive karmic reserves, ensuring a brighter future.

Self-Reflection and Intentional Living

<u>Awareness:</u> To harness the power of universal reflection, we must cultivate self-awareness. Reflect on your thoughts, emotions, and actions. Are they aligned with the energy you wish to attract?

<u>Intention:</u> Set clear intentions. Visualize the outcomes you desire. When you send out positive energy intentionally, the universe responds accordingly.

<u>Gratitude:</u> Gratefulness amplifies positive reflections. Acknowledge the blessings you receive, reinforcing the cycle of abundance.

The principle of universal reflection invites us to be conscious creators of our reality. As we navigate life's labyrinth, let us remember that our deeds resonate across the cosmic expanse. Choose kindness, sow seeds of love, and watch as the universe mirrors your intentions. Whether it's a gentle echo or a resounding symphony, our actions shape the cosmic dance.

In this grand theatre of existence, may our reflections be luminous, casting light upon our path.

Conscious Creation

In the vast cosmic tapestry, our thoughts, emotions, and actions resonate like celestial harmonies. The principle of universal reflection asserts that the energy we emit—whether positive or negative—ripples through the fabric of existence, shaping our reality. In this segment, we explore the profound impact of intention, gratitude, and conscious creation on our lives.

Setting Clear Intentions.

The Power of Focus: Our intentions act as cosmic beacons. When we set clear goals, we direct our energy toward specific outcomes. Just as a magnifying glass concentrates sunlight into a single point, intention focuses our creative force.

Visualization: Close your eyes and envision your desired reality. See it vividly—the joy, abundance, and fulfillment. The universe responds to this mental blueprint, aligning circumstances to match your vision.

Positive Energy and Cosmic Echoes

Sending Vibrations: Every thought and emotion emits vibrations. Positive energy resonates with the universe, attracting similar frequencies. When you intentionally radiate kindness, love, and compassion, these vibrations echo back.

The Ripple Effect: Imagine dropping a pebble into a still pond. The ripples expand outward, touching distant shores. Similarly, our positive actions create ripples of goodwill. A smile shared today may inspire acts of kindness tomorrow.

Gratitude: Amplifying Reflections

<u>The Grateful Heart:</u> Gratitude is a cosmic amplifier. When we acknowledge blessings—whether small or grand—we amplify their impact. Gratefulness opens channels for abundance. It's like tuning our radio to receive stations of joy.

<u>The Cycle of Abundance:</u> Gratitude perpetuates itself. As you express thanks, the universe responds by showering more blessings. It's not mere politeness; it's an energetic exchange. Gratitude fuels the cycle of abundance.

Conscious Creation

<u>Architects of Reality:</u> We are not passive observers; we are architects of our reality. Our thoughts mold the clay of existence. Be deliberate in your mental blueprints. What reality are you constructing?

<u>Alignment:</u> Align your intentions with your values. If you seek love, be loving. If you desire success, act as if success is already yours. The universe mirrors your inner state.

<u>Responsibility:</u> Conscious creation carries responsibility. Negative intentions also echo. Be mindful of what you sow. If you plant seeds of enmity, expect an acrimonious harvest.

The principle of universal reflection invites us to dance with the cosmos. Our intentions ripple through time and space, shaping our destiny. Set intentions like stardust, sprinkle gratitude like cosmic confetti, and watch as the universe responds. We are not victims; we are co-creators. As you read these words, remember: you are weaving constellations with your thoughts. "As above, so below."

This awareness is a big part of **The Chi Key** – Unlock your full potential!

Life does come with a built-in instruction manual! You now have the tools to better understand yourself and the world around you.

Knowledge Is Power And Power Changes Ones Destiny In Any Sphere Of Life

The more you work with the UNIVERSALISM truth of NUMBERS and VIBRATIONS, the more you will be enlightened, emboldened, and excited about grasping life and living the life you are here to live!

UNLOCK THE MYSTERIES of Existence with "The Chi Key"!

Remember this truth: Knowledge is power. It shapes destinies, bends realities, and weaves constellations. The Chi Key is your cosmic wand—wave it boldly!

Embrace the Universe Within. Your destiny awaits!

Follow J Pilgrim to get copies of his published books on topics like Wellness, Natural Therapies, and Philosophy.

Involved in the Internal Arts since 2005, he is a graduate of various internal art forms, including Thai Massage, and has knowledge in Reflexology, Gemstones, Numerology, and Nutrition.

He is also a certified instructor in Tai Chi and Easy Fitness programs.

As an author, he has books in online bookstores.

https://xcelbooks.weebly.com

Also by J Pilgrim

The Trionian Saga
The Trionian Saga - Part One: Beyond the Border Mountains
The Trionian Saga - Part Two: The Hyna Sword
The Trionian Saga - Part Three: The Quest for Lyla
Kass Balou

Standalone
The Hens in Poultsville
Sleeping with Crystal
Excel Your Wellness: Virtues and Vitamins
The Chi Key
Body Strengthening Strategy
Xcel Wellness Tai Chi
The Trionian Saga
Sherleaf
Endless Waterfall

Watch for more at www.thetrioniansaga.weebly.com.

About the Author

<u>Meet J Pilgrim</u>This renowned author has engaged readers worldwide with his published books on philosophy, wellness, and fiction. His portfolio of eBooks and printed works is available at all good online bookstores.His works delve deep into the human spirit, exploring the profound questions that have intrigued thinkers for centuries. Through these writings, the author offers readers a chance to embark on their own journeys of self-discovery and enlightenment.Whether you're seeking profound philosophical insights, practical wellness advice, or an epic fantasy adventure, J Pilgrim has something to offer.<u>Connect with J Pilgrim</u>Stay updated on J Pilgrim's latest releases, and more by following him on Books2Read. Join a community of readers who are inspired, entertained, and transformed by the works of J Pilgrim.

Read more at www.thetrioniansaga.weebly.com.

About the Publisher

Xcel Wellness has eBooks published in online bookstores with themes such as wellness, natural therapies, and philosophy.

Involved in the Internal Arts since 2004, the author is certified in Thai Massage, Tai Chi, Fitness programs, and Reflexology.

The author has eBooks published in all good online stores.

Read more at www.xcelbooks.weebly.com.